SHROPSHIRE ECCENTRICS

George Glover has spent most of a long life in Shropshire.
He is the author of *Shropshire Curiosities* and co-author, with
J.J.H. Edmonds, of *Three Operettas*. A retired schoolmaster,
he is an Open University graduate and joint editor of the
West Shropshire Talking Newspaper for the Blind.

Dan Slater spent half a lifetime as a grower of fruit and
vegetables, and ten years broadcasting on the BBC's *On your
Farm* programme. Nowadays, he lives and walks among the
Shropshire hills, painting wild flowers in their landscapes.
He exhibits at Ludlow's Silk Top Hat Gallery.

for auntie Phyl and David

with love

George Glover

SHROPSHIRE
ECCENTRICS

George Glover

with drawings by
Dan Slater

ARCH

© George Glover 1991

Published by ARCH,
The Hope, Lyonshall,
Kington, Herefordshire HR5 3HT

Photoset in Mergenthaler Bembo
at Five Seasons Press, Madley, Hereford

Printed and bound in Great Britain
by Billings and Sons Limited, Worcester

British Library Catologuing in Publication Data
Glover, George
Shropshire eccentrics:
good, bad and bizarre characters fron the county's past
I. Title
920.04245
ISBN 0 947618 06 6

The Eccentrics

Acknowledgements

I would like to thank Mr Tony Carr and his staff at the Local Studies Library at Shrewsbury for their patient help in my researches and the Reverend Percy Cullum, David and Evi for welcome criticism and advice.

Preface

What is an eccentric? There are many definitions, none of them entirely satisfactory. My choice is simply the person who behaves in an unusual way. Examine the context of his behaviour, the historical frame, and the role the subject has adopted, or been forced into. Then, if the way he carries on is out of character or unpredictable, he may be categorised as an eccentric—particularly if he appears to believe that his unorthodox conduct is the only logical course in the circumstances.

Thousands of eccentrics all over the world must have lived their curious lives and now be totally forgotten. Hearsay has a limited life; if matters are not recorded they are eventually lost or at best distorted into legend. So most of my Shropshire eccentrics made an impression sufficient to prompt someone to write about them. In a number of cases they recorded their eccentricities themselves in letters, diaries and printed works. Some of their antics and attitudes are well known, others not. I hope their stories will interest and entertain the reader.

A BALL WHO WAS ALMOST ROUND

William Ball (1795-1852)

William Ball, given the nickname *John Bull* by his contemporaries, was an amiable fat man who worked as a puddler (a stirrer of molten iron) and then as a shingler (gravel-worker) at the Coalbrookdale Iron Works in the first half of the nineteenth century. Different authorities record his weight as anything between forty stones and twenty-two stones ten pounds. No doubt this variation was due in some degree to the fact that he regarded being weighed as unlucky, and was reluctant to step on to the scales. It is unlikely that anyone would have tried to bully him into it.

For he was reputedly a man of great strength. The evidence for this is that he was capable of lifting a lump of iron weighing nine hundredweights and putting it under the forge drop-hammer. He stood about five feet nine inches tall, which is not a lot above the average height, but was six feet or so around the body, three feet around just one thigh, and twenty inches around the arm.

He was born at Horsehay in 1795 and began work puddling at the age of eight, when he needed a platform to get at it. When he was fifty a piece of molten iron flew into one of his eyes, which put an end to his puddling. He died in 1852 and is buried in Doseley churchyard.

At the 1851 Crystal Palace Exhibition Ball was an object of wonder and admiration. The story goes that he travelled up to London by train, but being too wide for the carriage doors and too heavy for the seats he had to be accommodated in the guard's van.

Another anecdote describes how, when Alfred Darby was born, a carnival was arranged to take place in Horsehay. It was someone's cute idea to have the procession led by the largest and smallest men on the company's payroll. The two were required to head the parade on horseback. The diminutive Bernie Poole leapt easily on to the back of his small pony, but William needed the assistance of block and tackle to reach the saddle of the strong horse provided for him. Something went wrong with the lifting tackle, however. He was dropped on to the neck of the hapless horse, and both man and steed crashed to the ground.

William, despite his great size, was active, popular, and very good company. He was said to have had a merry sense of humour and to have been an interesting man to talk to. Despite the disadvantage of his huge bulk, he maintained an appropriately Falstaffian attitude towards life.

TWO ODD DOCTORS

Dr Beech of Shrewsbury (1719-1802)

Dr Beech was what we might nowadays call a fitness
fanatic. He was careful about his diet and fond of walking. He saw no reason why, if a man took good care
of his health, he should not live for ever. Ironically, his
love of walking led indirectly to his death at the age of
eighty-three. Stepping out from Ellesmere to Shrewsbury
he was caught in a heavy shower of rain which resulted
in his developing a severe cold which, according to one
chronicler, proved fatal.

He seems to have been extraordinarily fit. He once
walked from London to Shrewsbury in four days. A few
weeks before he died he covered on foot the seventeen
miles from Shrewsbury to Oswestry in three hours. To
the end of his long life he was able to leap and run with
the agility of a boy.

Mr Pritchard of Whittington (1670-1748)

The Whittington surgeon Edward Pritchard was a high-wayman in his spare time, one of the many Robin Hoods who seem to have flourished in Shropshire. A stalwart fellow, and reputedly a good surgeon, he and his wife, who dressed as a man, were members of a successful band of robbers. They were proud of never having committed murder. They gave a lot of their booty to the poor, and Pritchard often dispensed advice and medicine gratis to the under-privileged.

A member of the gang called Evans, who lived on Knockin Heath, was taken prisoner and conveyed with a strong escort to Shrewsbury. Pritchard followed and took lodgings in the town. He was determined to rescue Evans, and soon did so, but it never became publicly known how.

In time Pritchard retired from robbery and devoted himself to his apothecary's shop full-time. He died quietly in his bed at the age of seventy-eight.

[From an entry in the Whittington parish register]

THE VALIANT ADMIRAL FROM SHREWSBURY

John Benbow (1653-1702)

Brave Benbow, he set sail, for to fight, for to fi-i-ight,
Brave Benbow, he set sail, for to fight;
Brave Benbow, he set sail, in a fine and pleasant gale,
And the enemy he turned tail, in a fright, in a fright.

The naval encounter being recalled and celebrated in the song was a four-day battle in 1702 off the island of Jamaica, and the hero was Admiral John Benbow, born forty-nine years earlier at Coton Hill, Shrewsbury. It is said that the lad conceived an ambition to go to sea as a result of watching the river traffic pass his front door. So, uninterested in his father's trade of tanning, he lit out one day, hanging, according to folklore, the key of the front door in a tree. He joined the merchant navy and became in due course a master mariner.

In 1686 his ship was attacked by pirates in the Mediterranean. His crew fought valiantly and thirteen of the sea-robbers were killed. Benbow decided to have the corpses decapitated, so that he could take the heads home as trophies. They were plopped into a large barrel of brine to preserve them.

Making his way home, Benbow called at Cadiz, where he had business. For some reason, when he went ashore in full dress, he took with him a cabin-boy, Caesar, carrying the pirates' heads in a sack over his shoulder. The customs men of the day were curious.

'What've you got in there?' one of them asked.

'Salt provisions for my personal use', the captain is supposed to have replied, archly.

Pressed to exhibit the contents, Benbow pretended reluctance, but finally told the boy to tip them out on to the table. The Spaniards were surprised. Was Benbow really proposing to devour these revolting objects?

He told them the story of the pirates' attack. They too had suffered all too frequently at the hands of bloodthirsty pirates. The tale soon came to the ears of the King of Spain, who received Benbow in Madrid and gave him a handsome present of silver. When Benbow arrived home, King James gave him a commission in the Royal Navy.

After that there followed many years of naval warfare with the French. When Benbow returned from a famous victory at St Malo he was made an admiral. Back in Shrewsbury, he was feted royally in the town by the civic authorities.

Benbow's finest hour was yet to come. In the West Indies, in 1702, on his flagship *Breda*, he set about a superior French fleet. His captains took fright when they saw the strength of the enemy, and fled. Benbow, however, stood and fought with signal courage and tenacity until a broadside of chain-shot shattered one of his legs. Even then, he insisted on remaining on deck, slung in a hammock so that he could continue to direct operations. When the French fleet withdrew, *Breda* limped back to Port Royal. Benbow did not survive the crude surgery of his day. His body was buried in Kingston. A tablet in St Mary's church, Shrewsbury, serves as his memorial, and on the wall of Furrow's garage a glass-fronted case contains a very old key attached to what purports to be a part of the original tree.

A FIGHTING RUFFIAN FROM WEM

Joe Berks *(1771-1812)*

Joe Berks was a butcher by trade. Born in Wem, he found work when he grew up in Birmingham, where his physique and fighting propensities earned him the sobriquet of *the burly Brum*. Later, when he had moved on to London, he was called *the Woolwich butcher*.

Berks was more of a brawler than a boxer, but he never lacked ambition, or courage, or tenacity. Unfortunately, he developed a surly arrogance which made him generally unpopular. This unlovely trait was compounded by drink.

In 1801 the reigning English champion was nineteen-year-old Jem Belcher. Belcher was a spectator at a Wimbledon Common fight when Berks, the worse for drink, accosted him on his way back to his coach. He removed his smock and set about the champion with great vigour. Belcher called a halt so that he could take his own coat off, and the fight was resumed in earnest. At this point a sporting lord took note of the butcher's aggression and arranged for him to have professional training with a view to a rematch with the champion.

Berks trained hard for a time, and laid off the ale, but the contest, arranged to take place at Enfield, was postponed because Belcher was detained by the police.

The re-arranged scrap took place at Maidenhead a month later, and Berks was knocked out after half-an-hour. The next fight between them was ruined because of a dispute among the officials. The two contenders fought twice more, and on each occasion Berks was outclassed.

The next, unexpected development was that Belcher suffered an eye injury playing racquets. He had to retire from boxing, and the question of his successor arose.

Berks might well have inherited the crown had he not been so disagreeable. The sporting administrators decided that Berks should fight for it, and the retiring champion, as was the custom, was asked to nominate a challenger. This turned out to be one Henry Pearce, of Bristol.

Pearce beat him twice, over a total of thirty-nine rounds. Berks joined the Army and as a light infantry sergeant fought in the Peninsular War against Napoleon. He was killed in 1812 at Badajoz.

Arthur Conan Doyle immortalised Berks in the novel *Rodney Stone*. The battling butcher might have realised his ambition to become champion had he been able to keep himself sober.

BROOKES THE OLYMPIAN

Dr William Penny Brookes (1809-1895)

William Brookes was a doctor of medicine. He trained in
Padua and Paris, and came back home to Much Wenlock
to take over his father's practice on his death. In those
times local festivals were the occasions for a good deal of
drunkenness and hooliganism. In Much Wenlock it was the
local races in particular which gave rise to a certain amount
of mayhem and loutish behaviour.

Dr Brookes, anxious to raise the standards of young,
working-class people, physically, culturally, and morally,
founded the Wenlock Agricultural Reading Society in 1841.
An offshoot of this was the Wenlock Olympian Society,
whose first annual games took place in 1850.

By to-day's criteria some of the competitions appear
a little bizarre. They included races, it is true, but also
football, cricket, quoits, wheelbarrow races, and Chase
the Pig. Archery was soon added, and throwing the jav-
elin, and rifle-shooting, but the biggest attraction was the
tilting, where mounted riders in medieval costume had to
gallop along and thrust a lance through a ring suspended
from a bar. As the years went by the currently familiar
track and field events were added to the schedule—the
jumps, the hammer, and putting a weight of no less than
thirty-two lbs.

By 1860 the Games had become open to the nation. Not
many competitors from outside Shropshire came to take
part, but the meeting could attract between 4,000 and 5,000
spectators, most of whom came by rail.

Dr Brookes was indefatigable in seeking support for his
enterprises. One of his ambitions was the acceptance of

Physical Education as a school subject, which required Board of Education funding. This was achieved in 1895, the year of the doctor's death.

How much his activities contributed to the revival of the international Olympic Games is not clear. King George of Greece, it is said, had invited the enthusiastic William Brookes along for the revival. Brookes had lobbied hard for them, and had managed to persuade de Coubertin, generally credited with their revival, to visit the Wenlock Games in 1890, seven years before the first modern Olympics.

AN UNSCRUPULOUS SHROPSHIRE MONEYLENDER

Thomas Clarges (early nineteenth century)

This man inherited a good estate, which he dissipated at great speed, but was filled with such remorse at what he had done, and having narrowly escaped gaol, that he suddenly made a firm resolution to turn over a new leaf. In the management of the shattered remnant of his fortune he became the most extreme miser that ever existed.

He retired to a cottage on a hill that overlooked the bigger part of the estate he had sold, and made a decision that he would not rest until he had regained it. From then on he lived on nothing but refuse, wore second-hand clothes, or anything he could get hold of cheaply.

He lent money in small sums, at enormous interest, all over the country. He travelled on foot night and day to find farmers in distress so that he could buy their cattle, which he drove to market himself. He did odd jobs, bought and sold, made every penny he could and spent nothing. By degrees he scraped enough money together to begin to deal in mortgages. He looked for young heirs to finance at extravagant interest. Then he became an attorney, and fleeced everyone who came into his clutches.

He lent money on his former estate, and then ceased to practise. For not only did he regain the estate, but he cheated the owner of more than £1,000. He was able to add to it almost every year, ruining hundreds by his tricks and stratagems. It was noticed that nobody borrowed money from him who did not eventually regret it. But he lent so easily that every day a number were tempted.

He arranged claims by distant relatives against half the estates in the neighbourhood, and after causing alarm and confusion by involving the owners in litigation, bought the properties cheaply himself. In brief, by a series of transactions incredible to those who did not know him, he amassed a personal fortune of more than £20,000. At the same time, while in possession of that (for these times) immense sum, he spent no more on all sorts of personal and domestic expenses than £62 a year.

[Paraphrased from *The Universal Magazine* of April 1874.]

THE WHITCHURCH TRANSPORTEE
WHO MADE IT BACK HOME

Thomas Cook (1811-?)

In 1831 Thomas Cook, of Whitchurch, an attorney's clerk, was found guilty of writing a letter to a William Churton, threatening to murder him and destroy his property. The letter ran as follows—

Churton,

We, men of determination, firm, resolute and undeviating, now without scruple are determined that your property shall not be of long duration, nor yet your existence: property got through roguery —Roguery, Churton, has been your constant practice since you were first established in life. Mark, therefore, the time is at hand when your blood shall atone for your rash and untoward acts. We will waylay your body and bring your family to total subversion which you know you well deserve.

We are, etc., etc.,
Men determined to right the oppressed,
Agents to Swing, London.

P.S. We give you this timely notice, in order that you may prepare for that last awful but sure end which awaits you.

Probably because of the social unrest in country districts at that time, and particularly in view of the rick-burning which was commonplace around Whitchurch, Cook was sentenced to transportation for fourteen years.

He was of better than average intelligence, and he was charged together with a forty-seven-year-old tailor named Richardson, who was married and had nine children. The tailor spoke fawningly to the court, blamed Cook for his predicament, and begged for mercy because of his family. He was given only two years' imprisonment. Cook, on the other hand, tried to read a long speech in court. The prosecutor claimed it was libellous, and the accused refused to continue.

Cook was sentenced to transportation, and shipped to New South Wales. At first he had to endure hard labour, road-making and other back-breaking tasks. But soon it was realised that he was educated and bright, and he found himself working in a government office in Sydney.

Later he was sent to Port Macquarie on the west coast, where he escaped. He was re-taken, and given a life sentence on Norfolk Island. There was no worse place in the colony.

As it happened a new governor, Captain Maconochie, who was of a more kindly disposition than his predecessor, took charge of the settlement. He formed a high opinion of Cook's abilities and made him a supervisor.

From then on he behaved himself so well that he was sent back to Sydney, and then to Port Macquarie, where conditions had much improved. But Cook, wearied of prison life, absconded once again. Somehow he was able to escape once more and make his way back to Britain.

During part of his enforced sojourn in Australia he had kept a diary. In England he got in touch with Captain Maconochie again and let him have the diary. It fell eventually into the hands of a London bookseller, who sold it in 1929 to a Sydney library.

Where Cook ended up is anybody's guess. There is some evidence that he settled down in France, returning only briefly to Whitchurch.

THE SCIENTIST WITH NOVEL THEORIES

Charles Darwin (1809-1882)

One of Shrewsbury's most famous sons had some difficulty deciding what he wanted to do in life. He was disinclined to enter his uncle Josiah Wedgwood's pottery business. After two years studying medicine and surgery in Edinburgh he decided he was too squeamish to enter his father's profession and become a doctor. He went to Cambridge, intending to train as a parson, graduated, and found himself drawn towards natural science. Then Professor Henslow aroused in him an interest in geology and recommended that he join the round-the-world voyage of scientific discovery being sponsored by the Government and led by Captain Fitzroy.

Darwin's father was opposed to this proposal but his uncle, who had observed and noted Charles's intense and sustained interest in plants and animals, supported it and the young man was given parental blessing.

Like Nelson, Darwin was always prone to seasickness. But he was fascinated by the observations and experiments made during the five-year voyage on the *Beagle*. Whereas he was never a quick learner, he was an accurate observer and a meticulous compiler of notes. In the Galapagos Islands he collected finches, giant tortoises and other animals, all of which helped to inspire the thought leading to the formation of his evolutionary theories.

He married his cousin Emma Wedgwood in 1839, and although never truly a fit man, he fathered ten children. *The Origin of the Species* appeared in 1859, and gave rise to violent controversy, especially among church leaders, some of whom felt that it was an attack on the Biblical account of the Creation. Certainly the work challenged thought, belief and received wisdom in the field of human biology.

Darwin always maintained that he was not an atheist and had not set out to undermine the basis of religious belief. He had merely published the results of his scientific enquiries. It was left to others to draw their own inferences.

From 1842 Darwin lived in Kent. His health was not robust. One acquaintance remembered his taking exercise by walking a gravel track around a 1½ acre field which formed part of his domain. Pacing around this 'sand walk', he would kick a stone from the side of the path on each circuit to keep count of the distance he had covered.

He died in 1882, having reached the good age of seventy-three. A Shrewsbury writer of that time was demanding to know why no public memorial had been erected in the town of his birth. A statue put up in London had attracted subscriptions from all over the world.

The matter was put right, of course. There are those who claim that along with Marx and Freud, Darwin was one of the greatest thinkers of the nineteenth century.

THE STRANGE MASTER OF TONG CASTLE

George Durant (1776-1844)

For nearly a hundred years Tong Castle was the home of the Durant family. There were four consecutive heads of the family called George. The first had made a fortune when he was clerk to the British Forces in the West Indies. He bought Tong Castle and concentrated on rebuilding it in Moorish-Gothic style and in creating a lake in the grounds, advised by the one-and-only Capability Brown.

Our subject, George Durant the second, inherited the estate at the age of twenty-one. The house and grounds being more or less finished, the new owner bent his energies towards the building of a number of exceedingly weird adjuncts to the estate. A few of these remained, long after the castle has been demolished. They included an impressive gateway, and near it a summerhouse, or pulpit, where the squire could sit and talk to passing friends. He built an Egyptian hen-pen, sporting many odd inscriptions and pictures, a dove house, an ornamental pigsty and a pyramid.

A hermitage was created, and supplied with a resident hermit, who lived there for seven years. His less durable successor, an ex-soldier, lasted only one month.

Aeolian harps made of iron were mounted on pillars in the wood, so that the wind soughing through them would terrify and drive away sensitive poachers. An archway of whales' jawbones was erected.

Perhaps the most inventive of these toys was the iron weeping willow which contained hidden pipes. In the same spirit as the water-works in the Austrian castle at Hellbrunn, the unwary visitor could be thoroughly drenched by sitting on the seat beneath the 'tree'.

George II had two wives. The first left him in 1817, divorcing him, and successfully claiming alimony of £600 a year. George contested this, had the sum reduced to £200, and celebrated by erecting a hideous monument within sight of the castle—a monument which two of his sons blew up with seventy pounds of explosive on the night he died.

The first Mrs Durant bore him fourteen children, but despite her apparent compliance with his demands he 'left the Royal Feast to prey on the Garbage'. He is reputed to have fathered thirty-two illegitimate children in the village. The dovecote and the laundry appear to have been the scene of many of his clandestine activities. To be fair to him, he took quite an interest in his offspring, standing godfather to them and giving them euphonious names, of which Columbia Cherrington, Napoleon Wedge and Cinderella Greatback are examples. The story is told that one of his wives spotted a smoking chimney in a wing of the castle she had never visited. Comfortably ensconced around the hearth were one of her husband's mistresses and their three children.

Durant's family life was always abrasive. A grim tale tells how he determined that his seven-year-old son should learn to swim by being flung, fully clothed, into the lake. He drowned.

When his eldest son George went to the continent and married without telling his father, his allowance was abruptly cut off. He never returned to Tong, and pre-deceased his father.

When George felt his end approaching he instructed the master carpenter to make him a coffin of Spanish mahogany suitably adorned with the family arms. His widowed second wife Celeste soon moved away from Tong and another, more rational George Durant took charge of the estate.

A SHROPSHIRE GIANT

Thomas Dutton (1853-1926)

Thomas Dutton was one of the celebrated Shropshire Giants, but whereas Billy Ball (*q.v.*) worked in a factory and Edmund Cornewall was a soldier, Dutton belonged to the land. He left the farming scene to capitalise on his size. His height of seven feet three inches earned him a living first as a commissionaire and then as a freak exhibit in a circus. At home in Longdon-on-Tern, he played an important part in the rebuilding of the local church, manhandling on the site the massive stones used in the construction of the tower. He also carried six hundredweight of corn around a barn for a bet.

As an agricultural worker he would have been a valuable asset to any farmer. Apart from being able and willing to hump about three times as much weight as the average labourer, he reckoned to mow a field of 3¾ acres with a scythe in nine hours. He was a good hedger and ditcher, but needed tools specially made for him, with handles of unusual length and thickness.

His job of commisssionaire, carried out wearing a morning suit and a top hat, was outside Lewis's, in Manchester. People were drawn to the shop just to see this imposing giant.

With Wombwell's circus he was tricked out in quasi-military garb, holding a spear, and was labelled the British Soldier Giant. This job enabled him to travel all over Europe, including seven years in France. On tour he learnt to be a competent tailor and saddler, though mending children's shoes posed problems because he couldn't get his huge hands inside them.

In Manchester, he married Betsy Allmark from Hodnet. We are not told how tall she was but she appears in a photograph to be of normal height. She bore Thomas several children.

Though he was friendly and harmless, his very size intimidated the village children, who used to scurry away to a safe place when they saw him approaching. A local man once rode down to Bristol with Thomas on the train, and paid a shilling to enter the circus, only to find that his travelling companion was the prize exhibit.

Thomas retired from the circus when he felt himself growing old and had become tired of the nomadic life. He died at seventy-three, having enjoyed life to the full.

THE UNPREDICTABLE RECTOR
OF WHITCHURCH AND MYDDLE

Francis Egerton (1756-1829)

After a brilliant academic career, the Reverend Francis Egerton was ordained at the age of twenty-four, and became Rector of Whitchurch and Myddle in the following year. Although he held the two livings for nearly half a century, he spent little time in Shropshire and in 1817, when he was sixty, he bought a large residence in Paris and left England for good.

When he did live in Whitchurch he behaved like the contemporary squarson, a mixture of squire and parson, hunting and shooting over his estates around Ellesmere, and entertaining lavishly. A wealthy man in his own right, he received a combined stipend of some £3000 for his two parishes, but employed three curates at Whitchurch to minister to his flock.

His moral standards were questionable for a man in holy orders. He was believed to be responsible for five illegitimate children, all girls, but nobody seemed to know how many mistresses were involved. Four of the five did not survive childhood; the fifth, named Sophia Cotton, was brought up by him and lived with him.

At one stage Egerton crossed swords with a local barrister named Wickstead. So virulent did his hate become that he passed around to his friends copies of a picture illustrating the bizarre steps he had taken to torment his enemy. It shows one of his fields in front of Wickstead's house, littered with unsightly piles of planks, a tethered fox and dog, a bell, a wind-driven propeller attached to a rattle, bones from the slaughterhouse, and a man busy sharpening cross-cut saws.

The fox made the dog bark, the agitated dog rang the bell. The propeller shook the rattle, the burning bones stank, the saw-sharpener produced a continual teeth-juddering rasp. This pernicious assault on the barrister's senses led to a court action which cost Egerton so much in damages that he was forced to sell the field.

In late middle age Egerton suffered from a growth in his mouth which made his jaw stick out, affecting his appearance and his speech. He spent a great deal of his time writing scholarly treatises, in particular on Greek poetry, but during these years he became exceptionally eccentric.

His brother died in 1823 and Egerton became eighth (and, as it turned out, last) Earl of Bridgewater. He was so delighted with his new rank that he had his coat-of-arms put on every household article that would carry it, including the dog-collars. He took to being accompanied everywhere by servants in livery, and is said to have returned a book he had borrowed in his carriage with four attendant footmen.

He had a different pair of boots for every day of the year. Even his dogs had boots specially made for them. Two of these animals used to eat at his table, dressed in human clothes, and waited upon by footmen. If one misbehaved, he was banished to the servants' quarters and dressed in livery, being replaced by a more decorous dog with better table manners.

Egerton's jaw trouble took him into a lawsuit with a French dentist who had made him seven sets of ill-fitting teeth. This action he won, but was awarded only about one-third of the damages he had claimed.

Egerton's will revealed a redeeming generosity. He left £2,000 to the poor of Myddle and the same amount to the Whitchurch poor. £8,000 was made available for a literary competition and more funds went towards the church library at Myddle.

A ROMANTIC, MURDERING DESPERADO

John Evans (1801-1829)

John Evans was a young man, strong, agile and resourceful. He was good at his trade, which involved not only breaking, entering and stealing throughout the Welsh Marches, but also the passing of counterfeit money.

When he was resting from his unlawful occupations he called himself Squire Smallman. The proceeds of his shady endeavours enabled him to settle down for a time in Montgomeryshire, and pass himself off as a sporting gentleman.

One night in a pub his tongue was loosened with ale, and his indiscreet boasting led to his arrest and lodgement in Hereford gaol. While he was there, his parents' home at Pencoed was searched. So many neatly-packed stolen items were discovered there that his father and mother were conveyed to Hereford gaol to join their son.

Evans escaped by outwitting the gaoler. Leaving the exercise-yard first he nipped smartly up the steps to the upper landing before the turnkey joined the group. He wasn't missed. When things had settled down he wrenched two iron bars from a window and levered out bricks above the door to allow him to wriggle through and up into the roof space. Then he crawled across to the opposite side of the gaol and departed down the traditional rope of knotted sheets.

A few days later he turned up in a pub at Bishops Castle. Aware of the recent gaol break and suspicious of the stranger, a pub regular spoke to the landlord. Uneasy, Evans took his leave. But the regular, one Edward Richards, tackled him just outside the door, whereupon Evans produced a pistol and shot him in the chest. In the ensuing hubbub Evans made good his escape.

Richards recovered, £100 reward was offered for the capture of the miscreant, and two more robberies were reported, one at Churchstoke and a second at a stable, where a grey horse was stolen.

Eventually, the fugitive was cornered at the house of a Mr Wilson on Vowchurch Common. The law officers took Evans and Wilson, and the two were tied together and literally carted to Hereford. The news of the capture had spread so fast that at the bridge entrance to the city the crowd had to be moved to make way for the conveyance.

Evans was indicted for attempted murder at the Shropshire Assizes, and the Bishops Castle landlord, Richard Norton, described how the prisoner had in the past been to his pub several times on horseback, dressed in his alternative role of the landed Squire Smallman.

When his sister visited him in gaol before his execution he explained to her how he had picked locks with a tool made from a goose quill, and he claimed that he'd done no physical harm to anyone until the Richards incident. One of his last requests was that his sister return a gun he had stolen to its lawful owner. He knew that the man was particularly fond of it.

THE UNORTHODOX LINGUIST
OF STANLEY LANE

Gavin Gibbons (1922-1978)

The Meole Brace area of Shrewsbury has had less human interest since the lamentably early death of one of its best-known citizens, Gavin Gibbons. His father was a barrister and had been headmaster of Oswestry High School for Boys for many years. Gavin chose to be an author and a linguist. After Cambridge he worked for a publisher producing maps and travel guides, then decided to freelance. The subjects of his books naturally reflected some of his many interests—flying saucers, travel and languages. He preferred to collect topographical material by bicycle.

Gavin displayed an almost schoolboy fascination with railways and telephones, and his garden in Stanley Lane contained several objects connected with these interests— buffers, a miniature telephone system and a telephone pole, obtained by negotiation with what was then the G.P.O. His outlook commanded a view of a section of the permanent way leading from Shrewsbury to Welshpool. It is not the busiest track in the world, nor even in Shropshire, but apparently he got a thrill every morning watching the odd train crossing his line of vision.

His published guide *Welsh Border, the Wirral to the Wye* is well-written, containing much detail other guide-compilers might have considered not worthy of inclusion. An unusual feature is that the author mentions himself in the text six times, his father, his wife and his family once each.

Gavin, who once told a reporter that he was mastering his eleventh language, married a Scottish lady, also a confessed linguist, in 1963. He gave her a bicycle instead of an engagement ring.

It could never be claimed that Gavin Gibbons was averse to being noticed. He was accustomed on occasion to carry a handbag, maintaining that he needed it to hold his bits and pieces, and wear a headscarf, necessary, he would say, for keeping his head warm. Other men, he would imply, would do well to stop their ill-informed jibes, and follow his example.

He was a regular writer of letters to the newspapers, most of which created interest and comment, and an indefatigable conversationalist. No train journey with Gavin for company could ever be dull, or provide time for contemplation.

Perhaps his finest hour was when he paid off his mortgage dues after a fair amount of hassle with the Building Society concerned. Priming the local media beforehand, he approached the office with his contribution in coppers, bowling it in a wheelbarrow along High Street.

He classed himself as a flourishing individualist. He certainly enriched the domestic life of the town.

AN AGRICULTURAL FACTOTUM

Bill Goode (1900?-1980?)

Bill was a well-known character in a village on the border of Wales. Everybody in the locality knew who was meant by 'owd Bill'. His eccentricities gave a spice to daily life, which could, in all conscience, be dull enough.

A stiff little fellow, as he was described, he served his term of years with the colours with the British Army, mostly in India. He returned to civvy street with a straight back, a purposeful step, a foul tongue, and a not-too-secure relationship with the truth.

Bill couldn't seem to settle after his Army travels. He made himself available for casual farm work, to augment his pension, and his total income was sufficient to satisfy his modest bachelor demands. Ale was his basic need, more important than regular meals, and Woodbines, which he ceased to smoke only when eating or asleep.

He wasn't a bad worker, but without finesse or pride in what he did. He used to remark that he would never be recommended for the agricultural medal, so he was aware of his limitations.

In the winter he could be seen topping and tailing sugar-beet, a soul-destroying job, often spending the whole day, solitary as the Highland lass, in a twelve-acre field, hacking off the leaves and roots of the beet with a 'brummock' (broom-hook). He would continue to chop away in heavy rain, only a hessian sack to protect his shoulders.

When the ground was dry enough he would be spreading manure at a penny a ruck, a job that required a certain twist of the wrist to achieve an even distribution. Come harvest-time he was in great demand. After the harvest came the thistling, when he wandered lonely as a cloud over grazing meadows, slicing off the spiky leaves and purple heads with his flashing scythe. Often he would be doing the job too late in the year and the air would already be full of downy parachutes.

Bill was a 'dab hand', he claimed, at the 'hedge-brushing', then, of course, done with a sickle or, in the case of an over-grown hedge, with a long-handled 'slasher'. When under observation by passing pedestrians, Bill's sense of theatre would lead him to wield this tool so flamboyantly that the severed ends of hazel, holly and hawthorn flew for yards and the sweat oozed down his throbbing temples. Most people knew not to stand in line with the arc of the whirling hook, for it sometimes slipped out of Bill's tiring grasp.

Hedging and ditching were the last of his basic skills, entailing bloodletting at the barbed wire and slopping through trenches full of gluey mud. In between the main seasonal occupations Bill was free to take on anything earthy, from winter digging a widow's plot to emptying the revolting cess-pit behind the village school.

As he grew older and work on the ranch became too much for him, Bill took a job as general factotum at the knacker's yard. Frequently, on his way home, weaving on foot or swaying on his bicycle—for he could never pass a pub—he'd meet a herd of cows being driven along the road. They must have been able to smell blood on his clothes, for the normally placid, shambling beasts would make for him, and he'd have to take refuge behind a hedge or in a handy telephone kiosk. He had words for these occasions. They tended to be repetitive and not at all nice.

THE CONDOVER CHINA COLLECTOR

Thomas Gosnell (early nineteenth century)

Thomas Gosnell lived with his sister in a house in Condover which had been in the family for many years.

His physical appearance tended to attract attention. In figure he 'was not easily forgotten. Of medium height, rather corpulent, his clothes ill-fitted, his silver buckled shoes, unbraced knee breeches, and broad-brimmed slouching Leghorn hat, at once stamped him as an eccentricity of no ordinary description.'

'He was a great adept in culinary matters,' we are told by another correspondent to the *Shrewsbury Journal*. 'Cooking occupied most of his time.' But he was best remembered as a collector of curiosities, mainly of the china variety, and dolls, or puppets. He left an extraordinary collection of old pots. There were scent-jars, tea-pots, tea and coffee cups, cream ewers, basins, saucers, plates, punch bowls, jugs, mugs, mostly antique and curious, and including a 'pickle stand of seven compartments, ornamented with shells and other devices', and 'three mandarin choristers'.

The dolls were similar to the 'peripatetic Punch and Judy', and Mr Gosnell enjoyed entertaining children with these, to their great glee. His collection also included oil paintings, specimens of needlework and five large brass dishes some two feet in diameter.

Gosnell was 'very weak and uneducated', very superstitious, and was so fearful of demons and bogeys that he wouldn't sleep in his room without company. We are not told how this problem was resolved. He had great faith in charms, and one correspondent described the collector's method of getting rid of warts.

'On one occasion, when very young', he wrote, 'I was coaxed into letting him perform on a large, unsightly wart on my right hand. On going to him he produced a huge carving-knife, shaped like a scimitar, which he solemnly proceeded to sharpen with a steel, at the same time pronouncing some unintelligible gibberish. Of course I was very much alarmed, and naturally shrank from the ordeal, but being reassured by an accompanying relative, reluctantly yielded. He then repeated some incantation which I cannot remember, made the form of a cross on the wart with the aforesaid knife, and cut a piece of stick which he then threw away. I was then told the operation was over and the wart would soon go. Whether I had faith in the performance, or not, I cannot remember, but it is a fact that the wart disappeared suddenly and imperceptibly.'

Thomas Gosnell was buried on the north side of Condover churchyard, near what was then the new porch, but no stone was put up or laid down to mark the spot. The curious reason for this was believed by the villagers to be that the beneficiaries of his will did not care to perpetuate the name Gosnell.

A VILLAGE CHRONICLER

Richard Gough (1635-1723)

Richard Gough, yeoman farmer, was responsible for that most fascinating work of local history known as *The History of Myddle*, which is a pleasant working village about five miles north of Shrewsbury. When he started to write his manuscript, in 1700, Gough was a sixty-six-year-old widower. His family's long association with the district, combined with a sound private education, enabled him to put together an account which is full of interest and humour, and throws a great deal of light on life in rural England under the Tudors and Stuarts.

Our chronicler's record is in two parts. The first is a conventional description of the social structure of the district, valuable but not remarkable. For the second part, though, he made a plan of Myddle church, with its rigid allocation of pews to families—gentry, farmers and craftsmen, then cottagers. He considered each family in turn and gave details of its history, including gossip and scandal, which prevented publication of the manuscript for more than 100 years.

A couple of short examples convey the flavour of the work:

'Not long after this purchase, my uncle John Gough dyed; butt my aunt Katherine, survived him. Shee was soe extreeme fatt, that shee could not goe straite foreward through some of the inward doores in the house, butt did turne her body sidewayes; and yett shee would go up staires and downe againe, and too and fro in the house and yard as nimbly, and tread as light as a gyrl of 20 or 30 years of age.

'This Michael Chambre was whoally addicted to idlenesse, and therefore noe marvel that hee was lasciviouse . . .

'Butt the worst of this Michael was, that his lewd consorts were such ugly nasty bawds, that they might almost resemble uglinesse itselfe, and such as were the very scorne of the greatest and vilest debauchees of those times, of which, (the more the pity), there were too many in this parish. Soe prone is humane nature to all vice'.

Gough was a man of substance in the village. His knowledge of family history, not all of it a matter for pride, was extensive, his memory far-reaching. He wrote clearly and well; his humour leavened what might well have been a lump. There appears to be no bias in his conclusions. He dealt out praise and censure even-handedly.

Gough's wife died in 1694. She was buried in the church. Her epitaph reads:

> Too good to live with mee
> Not good enough with her to die

which seems to reflect the author's modesty.

He died at the venerable age of eighty-eight, not aware, perhaps, of the immense interest his writings would generate so long after his departure, and the value historians would come to place on them.

A SHIFTY, QUARRELSOME 'PARSON'

'The Reverend' L.H. Halloran (1764-1831)

Halloran was brought up an orphan, but managed to obtain a reasonably good education. He then forged documents to prove that he was in holy orders.

Sailing under false colours, as it were, didn't stop this excitable Irishman from falling out with everybody he met. He was a versatile fellow, with enough courage to maintain a high profile throughout the Battle of Trafalgar as a naval chaplain, and sufficient sensibility to publish seventeen volumes of verse and theology.

Exchanging life on the ocean wave for a post with land forces in Cape Town, he soon tangled with Governor Grey, and eventually found himself banished from the colony. On his return to England he became curate at Broseley, where he forged a postal frank, which meant that he had cheated the postmaster of tenpence. He might have got away with that had he not quarrelled with the rector.

Halloran had an exceptionally short temper, and was believed to always travel with loaded pistols about him. The two officers sent to arrest him were taking no chances, therefore, when they burst into his lodgings, tied him up, and hauled him off to Newgate. It was of no avail to protest that his pistol toting had been given up twelve months earlier.

Halloran's influential friends had seemed reluctant to help him, but public sympathy was on his side at his trial. Surprisingly, he pleaded guilty, claiming that his only witness had died. The real reason was that a cross-examination would have exposed his bogus claim to be an ordained clergyman. He was sentenced to transportation to New

South Wales and no amount of pleading and appeals to people in high places could save him. Someone in authority must have been aware of his true standing and been anxious to have him out of the way. Invalid marriages he had 'solemnized' coming to light could have caused many problems.

In Australia Halloran prospered as an educationalist, but created trouble wherever he went. A contact procured a ticket-of-leave for him but it was cancelled. He was criticised for not having a religious book of any kind in his school. Soon he was in prison again for debt.

Released, but still encumbered with debt, Halloran became in turn a newspaper proprietor and an estate agent. The paper soon failed, and the Governor made him Coroner for Sydney. A heart attack carried him off in 1831, still without the right to wear a clerical collar.

THE CONSCIENTIOUS COACHMAN

Sam Hayward (1805-1851)

Sam Hayward became famous round about 1830 as the flamboyant coachman who regularly drove his coach and six horses over the English Bridge and full tilt up the Cop, swinging without check through the arch into the courtyard of the Lion Hotel. His judgement had to be precise, for there were only inches to spare. It is not recorded that he ever miscalculated his approach.

Such a feat in so public a place was sufficient to ensure Hayward's niche in local legend. He was in charge of the 'Lion' run to London for many years. Only the arrival of the railway brought his career to an end.

His coach, the *Wonder*, was one of eleven operating from the inn, which had become celebrated under the proprietorship of Richard Laurence. The London coach could cover one hundred miles in a day. Horses were changed every eight miles or thereabouts, and the complete trip involved one hundred and fifty horses. The changeover gangs, in the interests of cutting journey time, could switch teams in less than a minute.

Hayward was noted for his fierce concentration on the job in hand, to the extent of being taciturn, even surly, with the passenger inclined to chat. He was once asked:

'What the devil ails you, Hayward? Are you dumb?'

His reply was: 'Can't drive and talk too!'

He was said to be capable of making the whole journey without a word.

Fiercely proud of his reputation, he reckoned never to be more than ten minutes late, a tolerance British Rail, over 150 years later and entirely unaffected by the abominable roads over which Hayward travelled, still regards as its target. If the public clocks didn't agree with the coach's advertised times, well, the clocks were often wrong, weren't they?

One of Sam's passengers, a lawyer travelling to Shrewsbury for the first time, felt a tremor of alarm as the horses launched themselves at a furious gallop at Wyle Cop. He touched Sam's sleeve. 'I think I'll get off here', he said.

'You be damned!' quoth Sam.

After his spell at the Lion, when the *Wonder* had begun to run to Birmingham Railway Station instead of to London —in 1842 it became a two-horse coach—Sam managed the 'Raven' and 'Bell' group. He died in 1851, and was buried in St Julian's churchyard beneath a flat gravestone. He had wanted folk to walk on his grave.

THE HODNET BOOK-COLLECTOR

Richard Heber (1774-1833)

Richard Heber of Hodnet, half-brother to the celebrated Bishop of Calcutta, was a bibliomaniac *par excellence*. He possessed the two necessities for book-madness: the sort of education which enabled him to appreciate and enjoy reading good quality books, and the wealth which made it possible for him to buy them.

He began by collecting in England, but after the end of the Napoleonic Wars his hunting-ground was extended to include France, Belgium and the Netherlands, where he bought property to house his ever-growing libraries. When he heard of a rare or unusual book, he could board a mail coach and go as far as four hundred miles to obtain it, not being prepared to trust agents.

He was no businessman when it came to acquiring a desirable volume. A Mr Brindley reckoned that he often picked up a rare book for a few shillings and sold it to Heber for more than its weight in silver and gold. A copy of Herbert's *Dick and Robin, with Songs and other tracts, 1641*, which he had bought for two shillings, he sold to Richard Heber for £10.

Heber had many duplicates in his collections. If friends commented on this, his reply was:

'Why, you see, sir, no man may do comfortably without three copies of a work. One he must have for a show copy, and he will probably keep it at his country house. Another he will keep for his own use and reference; and unless he is inclined to part with this, which is very inconvenient, or risk the injury of his best copy, he must needs have a third for the service of his friends.'

The Heber collection was the biggest in Europe. His Hodnet home was full of books. At his Pimlico house books were piled high in almost every room, on tables, chairs, and the floor. There were additional collections in Westminster, Oxford, Paris, Antwerp and Brussels.

After his death, the collections were broken up. The London auctions took 202 days, spread over two years. The catalogue ran to 2,000 printed octavo pages. Other sales were held abroad. They realised substantially less than Heber had paid out.

THE HARD-WORKING PARSON
FROM QUATFORD

The Rev. John Higgs (1675-1763)

John Higgs was the youngest son of a miller who lived in Claverley parish. He seems to have become the incumbent of Quatford in 1695, and never moved, so he was minister there for sixty eight years. Yet the stated income of the curacy was only £15 per annum. On this small living he raised a large family. He brought up his eldest son to be a clergyman and made over to him the perpetual advowson of Highley, worth at least £60 per annum, which he had bought. Another son he set up as a tanner, and his remaining sons in good trades. He left his daughter approaching £500 in money, land and houses.

To account for this miracle it should be understood that his wife, who died in 1718, brought some fortune to the union. His surplice fees at Quatford were at first considerable, especially for marriages, the village being in the neighbourhood of Bridgnorth and a popular place for the townspeople to go to be married before the Marriage Act of 1753.

He also obtained some tracts of land on the Common, which the inhabitants of Bridgnorth, who owned the royalty, permitted him to enclose and devote to agriculture.

He led the life of an anchorite, working on his little plots of land with his own hands, and making his children work harder, eat less well and go worse clad than the poorest labourer in the country. His own food and raiment were of the simplest and meanest. He and all his children were once found after a hard day's work sitting contentedly round a bowl of turnips with no addition except salt and bread. His best clothes were usually a plain black cloak made from the cloth with which his pulpit was sometimes hung for funerals. His ordinary clothes were the worn-out relics of his best, tied around his waist with a piece of cord. He often wore his cassock, which made it unnecessary to wear breeches; his clerical bands were frequently made of paper.

He was a primitive character living in a small house of his own built on the top of a romantic-looking rock. Around the house were many little caves, scooped out with his own hands, and devoted to different domestic uses. One he called his stable, another his hogsty, and so on, for sometimes he kept a little Welsh horse or a pig. At the foot of the rock he had hired workmen to sink him a well. After it was finished he began a flight of steps at some distance, and carried it down himself through the solid rock to the bottom of the well, where he made a little gallery and seats, where he often retreated in hot weather to sit and read.

He was a simple, pious fellow, a true ascetic, living to be nearly ninety. To the last he enjoyed all his faculties, being able to carry out all his duties to within a short time of his death. He was alert, nimble, and fit, and his face was smooth and healthy-looking. He was tall and thin, stooped, not from age but from hard work.

In his parish duties he was tireless. He never failed to attend at his church twice every Sunday and on every holy day, although divine service was obligatory only once a fortnight. His parishioners loved him as children their father. He would preach at any neighbouring church and go through the whole service for five shillings. He would walk to Astley Abbots (three miles from home) to preach there in the morning, go two miles further to preach at Tasley, and return to read prayers at Astley Abbots in the evening, all for a crown—this without appearing to be very tired, despite being over eighty, and having walked there and back.

AN INTREPID LADY

Florence Hunt (1843-1917)

Mrs Florence Hunt was the mother of the better-known Dame Agnes Hunt, the lady responsible, with Sir Robert Jones, for the founding and the fame of the Orthopaedic Hospital near Oswestry.

The family lived in a large house set in extensive grounds at Baschurch. Although not fond of children, Florence produced eleven in less than twenty years. They enjoyed all the benefits of a mansion, servants, and a park containing a lake, a cliff and a wood, but discipline was strict and could include a touch of the horse-whip.

When Mr Rowland Hunt died in 1879 his widow took the children to her own home in Leicestershire. There she heard a village hall lecturer suggesting that there was a fortune to be made breeding Angora goats in Australia. The intrepid Mrs Hunt decided that this was for her and off she went with her seven youngest children aboard the *SS Merwara* on the eleven-week voyage. It was a wretched trip, with bad weather and inadequate facilities, ending with the ship running aground off the Queensland coast. Prepared for the worst, Mrs Hunt put every stitch of her clothing on her sixteen-stone frame—and got stuck in the cabin doorway.

In Brisbane at last, no official had heard of the Angora goat breeding scheme. Unperturbed, Florence rented a house and found a horse and buggy. But when she and her eldest daughter Amy stood up in it their combined weight caused the floor to collapse and frightened the horse.

In her entertaining autobiography *This is my Life*, Dame Agnes described how her mother obtained incubators and set about establishing a chicken farm. A great many of the birds were born with a deformity of the legs. Mrs Hunt, equipped with a huge carving knife, operated on the hapless chickens with Agnes acting as anaesthetist. To help the patients to get about afterwards, Florence then fashioned prostheses out of large matches, but the birds were not grateful and struggled to kick them off.

Before returning to England, Florence decided to visit her eldest son Tom, at that time carving out for himself a station in the eucalyptus forest in Tasmania. After a dreadful journey, they found Tom living in a rat-infested shed next to a half-built bungalow, with no furniture or water-supply. Yet Florence insisted on a three-course cooked meal each night.

Despite the difficulties her obstinacy and odd ideas imposed upon her family, Florence's energy, enthusiasm and determination were important factors in the setting up and development of the care for the disabled in Shropshire which led to world-wide acclaim.

THE MISER OF BAYSTON HILL

William Jones (1779-1839)

'A person of the name of William Jones, aged sixty, who had been for a short time an in-patient of the Salop Infirmary, left there, at his own request, last Saturday week, being from the nature of his complaint considered incurable. When in the Infirmary he pleaded poverty to the extreme, but on the usual examination to see that his linen was clean, there dropped five shillings from his pocket, and on returning to him his coat there fell out thirty sovereigns more. The House-Surgeon therefore directed that a "Fly" should be ordered to convey him to his residence at Bayston Hill, near this town. On reaching that hamlet he called at "The Three Fishes", and was soon afterwards taken ill, and died on the Monday morning. It appears, however, that he told some of the persons who attended him that he had some money, and he directed them where it might be found in his cottage; on perceiving that they were going to examine it, he made an effort to grasp it, and in so doing he died.

'On an examination of his cottage not an article of furniture in the shape of a chair, table or bed was to be seen, but on pursuing the search nearly two hundred and forty pounds in gold, silver and copper was found, with securities for about £250. He seems to have been a wholesale collector of "inconsiderate (sic) trifles", for in addition to the above-mentioned, full half a peck of pocket knives, a score of pewter pots, with many articles of iron, chains, etc., an immense collection of old shoes, rags, various books, some in Latin, Greek and French, also presented themselves; in fact, everything that came his way he took care of.

'On a subsequent search yesterday, further securities on mortgage were discovered, to the amount of £250; besides this, he owned the cottage he lived in, and three other cottages in Bayston Hill, and claimed for common land on the adjacent waste.

'Thus he appears to have accumulated this property chiefly by begging and the sale of herbs, and sometimes by bringing to market a small collection of vegetables, which were always placed in a tolerably sized round basket.

'He has a brother and a sister now living; the former has been an inmate for some time in the Atcham Union Workhouse, the latter is a widow, residing near Newtown, Montgomeryshire, and who, with the children of a deceased brother, are the heirs of his thriftiness and penury—the latter was so strong as to refuse the person who drove him a glass of ale at the public house where he was left.

'His remains were deposited in Trinity churchyard, in this town.'

[Taken from a report in a Shrewsbury newspaper, January 1840]

A TROGLODYTIC ROBIN HOOD

Humphrey Kynaston (1470-1534)

Humphrey Kynaston remains one of Shropshire's favourite folk heroes partly because the concept of a Robin Hood figure plundering the rich to succour the poor is attractive, and partly because the outlaw's double-cave dwelling and the curving steps leading up to it are still readily accessible opposite 'The Three Pigeons' at Nesscliffe.

Kynaston, the son of a baronet, was keeper of Myddle Castle when he fell foul of authority.

His career as highwayman and benefactor of the poor did not last very long: he was pardoned after only a year. But that year was full of incident, with the prosperous wool-merchants afraid of him and the indigent of the district around Nesscliffe very much on his side.

Just as renowned as Kynaston was his horse Beelzebub, which lived in the second cave and was trained to mount the sandstone steps when summoned by his master's whistle.

Popular stories about the outlaw and his horse tell how Kynaston had Beelzebub's shoes put on backwards to confuse trackers. At least two attempts were made to capture this enterprising miscreant. The officers removed the central planks at Montford Bridge then waited for Kynaston to return from Shrewsbury. The outlaw, spotting what had been done, spurred on his steed to clear the gap. At first it was said to have been a chasm nine feet wide, but later chroniclers exaggerated it.

On the second occasion Kynaston had relieved a gentleman's steward of more than £500 and shared it, as usual, among his beneficiaries. Not long afterwards a letter from the gentleman was placed in his hands, informing him that the loss would force him to exact rent from poorer tenants who he normally allowed time to pay. This, he explained, would sully his reputation as a considerate landlord.

Kynaston checked up on this and found it to be true. His next move was to rob another estate steward, whose master he knew had no compunction about distraining upon tardy-paying tenants. He 'stripped him of every guinea, showing no compassion.' He then invited the first gentleman to a meeting, which took place in a quiet wood near Oswestry, and returned every farthing of his original haul.

These activities so incensed the authorities that all of the 120 constables in the district were assembled on a Monday, the day on which Kynaston was known to distribute lar-gesse to the poor. But when the constables approached Nesscliffe they perceived such a large crowd waiting for their benefactor that they turned and slunk silently away.

Kynaston eventually abandoned his short life of crime and settled down on a small estate near Welshpool, where he lived the life of an exemplary citizen until his death in 1534.

THE DIFFERENT VICAR

Rev. A.R.Lloyd (1817-1895)

The Reverend Albany Rossendals Lloyd, born at Whittington, was a son of the rector. He was educated at home, then at Trinity College, Cambridge. He was ordained in 1840, and became curate at Padiham, Lancashire and at St John's, Liverpool. His father had now become rector of Selattyn, and he put his son to act as the incumbent there. But when the father died, in 1851, a new rector was appointed and Selattyn had to be given up.

Mr Lloyd designed, built and mostly paid for the church of St Barnabas at Hengoed. Erected between 1849 and 1853, and now demolished, it had some odd features, including, inside, a window in the north transept with the rising sun above foliage and a strange inscription, and the pulpit and lectern very nearly as high as the roof. Outside, there were intimidating iron gates and a small, delicate spire with a bell turret.

The music was provided by a barrel organ played by a blind man. The hymns, composed by the incumbent, were printed in large type in books with a bright binding. In later life Mr Lloyd himself began to lose his sight. One Sunday when he was unable to find a certain text in the Bible he leant down from his lofty pulpit to ask a member of the congregation to find it for him.

He had a morbid dislike of candles. When visiting, he would forestall any move towards lighting candles by producing an oil-lamp with a request that it be used instead. In the winter it was his wont to place a light in his church spire on dark nights every Wednesday and Saturday, to light home those who had been to market in Oswestry. He used to ring the church bell at three o'clock every Saturday afternoon to remind his flock to polish their shoes ready for Sunday morning service.

He tried, and succeeded, in making his garden full of surprises, so that visitors would find the maximum pleasure and interest in it when he took them around. One of his mild practical jokes was a dark passage where the unwary would receive an electric shock.

THE WILLEY WHIPPER-IN

Tom Moody *(1756-1796)*

Tom Moody was universally regarded as the best whipper-in in all England. The job involved the management of a pack of hounds, under the control of the huntsman.

Tom, the son of a poor widow, was employed as a delivery-boy by a maltster in Broseley. One day, having delivered a couple of sacks of malt, he put his horse at a gate on his homeward journey. The horse refused. Tom tried him again and again until in the end the horse jumped it cleanly. Unknown to him, Tom was being watched by the local squire, George Forester, of Willey, who was so impressed by the boy's courage and perseverance that he found out who he was and then asked his master to release him to work at Willey Hall as a stable-boy.

A diligent pupil, Tom soon revealed unusual flair for working with horses. He eventually became whipper-in, and an admired favourite among local country folk. His fame spread far beyond the borders of Shropshire.

His weakness was an inordinate fondness for strong drink, and his popularity ensured that he was always copiously provided with ale. Regular and substantial intake of liquor rarely seemed to affect his ability to ride. He was never known to have been unseated.

His favourite watering-hole was 'The Hangman's Gate', between Bridgnorth and Much Wenlock, where travellers would leave their coaches to hear him tell stories of the hunt and sing popular ditties.

In appearance he was of average height, with small, lively eyes and a pock-marked face. In favourable conditions outdoors his high-pitched voice would carry a mile. He could not read or write, he never married, and he never made the rank of huntsman.

The time came when Mr Forester gave up keeping hounds, but Tom stayed with his old master. Worn out with hard work and excessive drinking Tom fell ill and died when only forty.

Mr Forester visited his favourite retainer, prepared to grant him any last wish within his gift. Tom requested a special burial ceremony. He wanted to be buried under a yew tree in Barrow churchyard, and to be borne to his grave by six earth-stoppers. His old horse was to follow, carrying all his hunting paraphernalia—the whip, boots, spurs and cap, and the brush of the last fox whose death Tom had attended. Four old hounds were also to form part of the cortege. Three view-halloos were to be given over his grave.

The celebrated entertainer Charles Dibdin marked the burial of the famous whipper-in with a popular song at Drury Lane:

> Thus Tom spoke his friends ere he gave up his breath,
> 'Since I see you're resolved to be in at the death,
> One favour bestow—'tis the last I shall crave,
> Give a rattling view-halloo thrice over my grave.
> And unless at that warning I lift up my head
> My boys, you can safely conclude I am dead!'
> Honest Tom was obeyed, and the shout rent the sky
> For everyone joined in the Tally-ho! cry.

He left twenty-six shillings.

THE BRIDGNORTH STARGAZER

Francis Moore (1657-1715)

Older people will remember *Old Moore's Almanac* as being a popular subject for discussion in the first quarter of this century. The predictions it carried were taken seriously by quite a number of people, but it was often difficult afterwards to find a real happening to fit even the vaguest forecast.

Francis Moore never lived to be old, for he died before reaching sixty. He was born in Bridgnorth but left Shropshire while still a young man and spent most of his life in London. He became assistant to a versatile but quarrelsome gentleman by the name of Partridge, who operated as the unlikely combination of shoemaker, astrologer, almanac-maker and physician. He had many detractors. Swift's epitaph was uncompromising:

> Here, five foot deep, lies on his back
> A cobbler, starmonger and quack,
> Who to the stars in pure goodwill
> Does to his best look upward still.
> Weep all ye customers who use
> His pills, his almanacs, or shoes.

Having taught himself to read and write, Moore went on to study medicine and obtain a licence to practise physic. Following Partridge's example, he earned a livelihood as a physician, astrologer, and schoolmaster, apparently omitting the cobbling.

Not much is known about Moore's character or personality. His portrait depicts him as fat in the face and wearing a full-bottomed wig. Moore's almanac, issued in 1699, showed the feast days of the church, but also advertised his goods and services commercially. Later came the weather forecasts and predictions of future events based on observations of the stars.

The almanac did well. Many people saw fit to study its pages before making any sort of plan. Next came the *Vox Stellarum*, or Voice of the Stars, another form of almanac, which met with substantial and sustained success. It was particularly well-regarded by countrywomen, but could also be found in town homes. Farmers were reported to be in the habit of consulting the almanac slyly before embarking upon any major agricultural enterprise, such as cutting the corn.

THE QUEEN OF THE HUNTER VALLEY

Mary (Molly) Morgan (1762-1835)

Molly Morgan from Diddlebury was probably the only lady to be transported to Australia twice. She was blessed with ebullient charm, a liking for men, and powerful larcenous tendencies.

Her adult life began conventionally enough. She married carpenter Morgan from Hopesay at twenty-three, bringing with her an illegitimate child by rich farmer Gough. Some time after she had had a second child, some missing bleaching yarn was found in the Morgan home. Her husband speedily slipped away, but Molly was apprehended. She was sentenced to transportation to serve fourteen years' imprisonment in Australia.

She was transported on the dreadful ship *Neptune*. A third of the passengers died on the way but Molly became popular with the crew, who protected her and gave her extra food.

Molly had spent three years at Parramatta when her husband appeared, somewhat surprisingly, as a free settler. Apparently he was unable to live without her. He obtained some land, set up as a carpenter, and she was allowed to join him. But her tendency to flirt with any personable man made him morose, and she decided to return to England alone. She worked her passage, in a manner of speaking, by accompanying the captain on the *Resolution* as his mistress. She was one of the few transportees to make it back to England.

Once home, she visited her children in Shropshire, then made her way back to Plymouth, where she 'married' a brass-founder named Mares. When that association turned sour she rewarded her new 'husband' by burning his house down and leaving for London, where she couldn't keep out of trouble for long. Either because she was hard up or because she was an incorrigible kleptomaniac, she pilfered some clothing. Once again she was put on a slow boat to New South Wales.

Molly served a further seven years in a convict settlement. There was no sign of her first husband and she never heard from him again. True to form, she found a mate, a man called Thomas Byrne, an Army sergeant. He provided her with a cabin and a little land to farm. Unhappily, some Government cattle were subsequently found on it, and she was banished to a camp at Newcastle.

She was able to charm Governor Macquarie as she had charmed most of the other men in her life. He granted her a ticket-of-leave, but she had to stay in Newcastle or in the valley of the Hunter River nearby. Now she began to deal in rum, which was popular with the pioneers but not with the authorities. Molly settled down in what is now West Maitland on the Hunter River and opened a pub to serve thirsty settlers. Her personality ensured that the place was a blooming success. She became rich and managed to acquire a third 'husband' (although the other two were probably still alive). He was Tom Hunt, a soldier, twenty years younger than she. Significantly, he changed his name to Morgan.

In 1823 the Governor of Brisbane gave Molly 159 acres surrounding her pub. Tom took over the bar and Molly, now in her sixties, set about farming with an energy similar to that of a later Mrs Hunt (q.v.) in Tasmania. She rode, shot, dug, fenced and built dams with the men, who included convict gangs lent her by the Governor. She bought another 600 acres of land, built a modern hotel in place of the crumbling inn, and was so liked and respected, partly as a result of the rum she so freely dispensed, that she was generally referred to as the Queen of the Hunter Valley.

THE OSWESTRY CONJUROR

Richard Morris (Dick Spot) (early nineteenth century)

Richard Morris, known to the populace as Dick Spot, was a celebrated conjuror in the Oswestry area. He was a 'professor of legerdemain' and a kind of astrologer, and was successful enough to have built up a good reputation. His fee for the hire of his skills was a piece of gold, payable in advance, failing which his talents could not produce results. Small wonder that in his maturer years he is reputed to have been 'in affluent circumstances' and to have 'kept his carriage'. The 'Dick Spot' nick-name related to a small-pox blemish on one side of his face.

He claimed that he was able to tell a lovelorn girl whom she would marry, to identify thieves by turning a key on a Bible, and to gladden the hearts of simple clients by predicting good luck and promotion for them.

Though he did not have the benefit of a formal education, Dick Spot was nevertheless an astute observer and judge of mankind. He was a tall, well-built fellow, with good manners and a natural dignity. He was most in demand for his opinion on property, whether it was stolen or not. His record seems to have been pretty good. It is probable that a thief would be informed when the conjuror had been called in, and, knowing his reputation for accuracy, would hasten to replace the goods before he could be called to account.

One night a gentleman living near Shrewsbury lost all his bed and table linen. Dick Spot, being in the vicinity, was summoned and paid. He listened to the sad tale with 'grave and fixed attention'.

'Sir,' he said at length, 'there is a person you suspect; but say nothing. Go home, and take no concern about your loss;

you will have it all again safe. I cannot tell you how, or when; but you will lose nothing.'

All the stolen goods were found, about fourteen days later, in a bundle, 'at daylight under his garden wall'.

For all his forecasting expertise, Richard did not foretell his own death. He was buried in Oswestry churchyard. Subsequently a churchwarden was asked for a pamphlet about the life of Dick Spot. Didn't know about his life, came the rejoinder, but he did have the man's remains, having bought the grave from Dick's granddaughter.

He had held the conjuror's skull in his hand only recently and had treated it with little more respect than the grave-digger had that of Yorick. If Richard Morris had had more reliable powers of clairvoyance, the man said, 'he would have ensured that his remains were placed in a less accessible spot.'

THE SQUIRE WHOSE EXCESSES
LED TO SELF-DESTRUCTION

Jack Mytton (1796-1834)

If you ask the average Salopian to name some Shropshire eccentrics the odds are that the very first offering will be Jack Mytton, the mad squire of Halston. His reputation in his day spread far and wide, way beyond the borders of his own county. He is said to have been extremely popular, especially with his tenants and servants.

He was born with a silver spoon in his mouth, and eventually inherited a large estate near Oswestry, and a fortune. By that time he had been thoroughly spoiled by an indulgent mother and expelled from two public schools. Discipline and self-control were never his strong suits.

In his favour it is always claimed that he was a good farmer and carried out sensible improvements on his estates. He was a skilled horseman, and many of the stories about him concern riding feats. There was no doubting his courage or his stamina. Once, with his arm in a sling, he leapt his one-eyed horse Baronet over the Attingham Park railings. To toughen up his horses for hunting, he rode them up and down staircases and steps.

In his time he served as Member of Parliament for Shrewsbury, Mayor of Oswestry and High Sheriff for Shropshire and Merioneth.

Many people will be familiar with the story of his misdeeds—his drunkenness, his gambling, and his practical jokes, which terrified people and made fools of his victims. He is said to have consumed between four and six bottles of port every day, and he laid preposterous wagers, succeeding in the end in running through his entire fortune, so that his land, his house, furniture and paintings had to be sold to pay off his debts.

The practical jokes are legendary—tipping people out of gigs, releasing foxes in the Lion Hotel, riding a bear into a crowded room. The most humiliating for his victims, perhaps, were when he forced his staff to skate and found the results hilarious. Another time he disguised himself as a tramp to test their reaction.

His outdoor feats were hare-brained enough to form the talk of the town—swimming large rivers and leaping over small ones, duck-shooting in winter in his night-shirt. Perhaps craziest of of all, he set fire to the tail of his shirt to cure himself of hiccups. Curiously, he seems to have been admired for these mad antics and his fame spread across the country.

The chickens came home to roost when he was still only in his thirties. Penniless and drink-sodden, he finished up a wreck in a debtors' prison, and died from a combination of ailments and miseries. His body was brought home for burial at Halston, and an enormous crowd lined the route to his grave.

THE WHIMSICAL HERMIT

Owd Sir (c.1825-c.1900)

The man known locally as 'Owd Sir' lived in a cottage backing on to a hillside in the neighbourhood of the Stiperstones. He was a retired miner who had never married, and he appeared to be quite content with his own company and that of his lurcher dog. He was fond of all animals and birds, and local people who came across a stray or injured creature and did not have the time to look after it tended to go to Owd Sir for advice. Often he'd take over the patient and nurse it back to health himself.

In those days, before farm mushrooms had been basic slagged out of existence, he knew the best places to look for them. Crops varied from year to year, but Owd Sir could be relied upon to know where the best pickings were, and also when was the best time to go. The black-faced miners were wont to make dawn raids on their way home from the pits and the children would quarter the fields as soon as school was out. Owd Sir had long ago learned how to pre-empt those two rival forces.

If you were naive enough to ask Owd Sir's advice as to the most likely place to find a capful, he'd direct you with a conspiratorial voice and a straight face. When you came back past his front door with a few miserable buttons, he'd show you the beautiful, clean, pink-fleshed mushrooms he'd managed to come across himself. Like the experienced grocer, he had always placed the best on the top.

He devised a whole range of practical jokes which he gleefully played on the locals. He was such a kindly fellow that few people ever bore him a grudge. A visitor could be asked if he'd mind threading a needle for Owd Sir, whose eyes were growing a bit dim. The Good Samaritan usually found difficulty in carrying out this modest request, and it would make him either puzzled or rather cross.

'Have you got your specs with you?' Owd Sir would enquire, po-faced.

The visitor would fumble around in his pockets, pull out his glasses and wedge them on his nose. Only then would he discover that the needle had no eye.

It was a piece of mischief on Owd Sir's part to set the hillside on fire, a ploy which caused no serious damage among the heather, broom and bracken but which generated alarm and the deployment of fire-fighting folk. Owd Sir's trick was to light a candle in a bottomless tin, place it in a suitable spot, and set off strolling over the hill. By the time the fire caught hold he'd be too far away from the seat of the blaze to qualify as a suspect.

Owd Sir was a regular member of the local chapel congregation. He was once asked to devise a competition to raise funds to pay for the winter fuel. A 'mystery parcel' was made up and Owd Sir's neighbour—for the old man was a touch shy about reading and writing—listed clues to the contents. You had to pay a small fee, and guess.

The clues were: 'Something a man can't do without', which was a shirt; 'Something a woman can't do without', which was a packet of tea; and 'Something a woman wears and her husband never sees', which was her widow's weeds.

Owd Sir's favourite hobby was following the hounds. Despite his age, he never seemed to grow tired of chasing up hill and down dale after the hunt. No doubt his local knowledge helped him to make the best use of short cuts, and maybe the best part of the day was the pint in the pub at the end of it, his pot usually being re-filled more than once by the locals, who had a soft spot for this mischievous but warm-hearted hermit.

THE LLANYBLODWELL PARSON
WHO TRANSFORMED HIS CHURCH

Rev. John Parker (1798-1860)

In the enchanting village of Llanyblodwell the Church of St Michael the Archangel, 'the church of flowers', is mute testimony to an eccentric parson, the Rev. John Parker. This gentleman was the incumbent there for only fifteen years in the middle of the nineteenth century, but he used a great deal of his time to 'restore' his church in a highly individual way.

Mr Parker was well-off, and deeply interested in architecture. Once he had gained the confidence of most of his parishioners, he was able to go ahead with a number of exciting renovations and improvements. At least, that's how Mr Parker must have seen it. He first restored the crumbling south wall of the church, built a porch and buttresses, a vestry and a tower. Then he went on to deal with the windows, the spire and the ceiling, among other projects.

He is reckoned to have spent £10,000 of his own money on the church and related buildings in the village. Of all this work, the spire, shaped like a torpedo, or a cigar, must have been the most difficult enterprise.

This vigorous and versatile vicar went on to improve the church interior, re-aligning the seating and installing a two-decker pulpit. After that he decorated in a most exuberant fashion. Rich colours were used for painting the roof and beam-ends; texts and inscriptions in colourful styles were freely applied throughout the interior, especially around the archways.

Not everybody agreed with what he had done, and some

of those who came after him undid much of his work. But in 1960 nearly all his 'restorations' were restored, and the results are there for all to see and to enjoy. The wild splendours of his unorthodox decorations give a vivid impression of the remarkable and eccentric John Parker.

A MAN OF LEGENDARY VIRILITY
AND AN INCREDIBLE LIFE-SPAN

Thomas Parr (1484-1635)

There are small discrepancies among the various authorities
as to the year of the old man's birth. Not surprising, since no
written record exists, and the approriate date was arrived at
by asking him who was on the throne when he was young.
There are those who believe that there were two Thomas
Parrs, father and son, who lived in the west Shropshire
hamlet of Winnington, and that they have become fused
in folk-memory into one incredibly old farm labourer.

This might explain how he was able to do a full day's
hard work at the age of one hundred and thirty, marry at
eighty and again at one hundred and twenty, and get a third
woman into trouble, as the saying used to go, when he was
one hundred and five.

He died in 1635, so if his date of birth is as stated he
lived in the reigns of ten sovereigns, from Edward IV to
Charles I. A plaque in Wollaston church gives the details.
He was buried, though, in Westminster Abbey.

Much of what we know about Parr is derived from
the verse of John Taylor, the 'water-poet', writing not
long after the old chap's death. Parr was the kind of
dedicated farm worker, apparently, who plods on from
daylight until dark, and has no interest in retirement.
Work was the only activity he knew, except for that
naughty affaire, and the poor man had to do penance for
that, standing for several hours in the porch of Alberbury
church, clad only in a white sheet at the age of one
hundred and five. Perhaps he thought it had been worth
it.

He ate, according to Taylor and others, rancid cheese, hard, coarse bread and onions. His beverages were milk, buttermilk, whey and water, with the occasional leather jug of ale, and cider or perry at weddings and fairs.

Some local historians have listed a number of later Parrs, allegedly descendants, who also lived to a great age. Others point out that the old man's two legitimate children died in infancy. One asserts that Parr was a heavy smoker; another states that he never smoked.

It was the Earl of Arundel, visiting his Shropshire estates, who heard about Parr and directed that he be brought to London for King Charles to meet—a long way at that age, one might think, to be carried to the capital on a litter. The escorting party got the maximum mileage out of exhibiting the old man, drawing considerable crowds on the way and at the inns where they spent each night.

Thomas couldn't think of much to say to the King when he got to London, it is reported, so the whole enterprise was perhaps a bit of a disappointment. Be that as it may, the effect of the long journey, the excitement, the stink of London and the unaccustomed rich food spelt the end of the road for Thomas Parr.

AN INDEPENDENT SPIRIT FROM LUDLOW

William Purslow (1800?-1882?)

'Lately died at Ludlow, at an advanced age, that eccentric character, William Purslow, self-titled esquire, well known to many persons, besides his neighbours, for having some years ago tamed two hedgehogs as to make them perambulate the streets with him, in a degree of discipline and subjection which astonished the beholders.

'In the early part of his life he was a soldier—served on the Rock of Gibraltar during its siege by the Spaniards. His latter years had been chiefly supported by the bounties of his opulent and benevolent neighbours.

'Though in the utmost degree of penury and wretchedness, he would never submit to receive parochial relief; and several years ago he had saved £7, which he deposited in custody of friends for the express purpose of defraying his funeral expenses; that even his interment might not be chargeable to the parish funds. Of this sum three-fourths remained untouched at the day of his death.

'His form was athletic, his constitution robust, and his features discovered a firm, heroic spirit. Had he been placed in more fortunate circumstances for the exhibition of that spirit, he would probably have been a hero of prominent merit.

'During several years past lameness, occasioned and confirmed by his hard manner of living, compelled him to hobble to eternity on crutches.

'In principle he was strictly honest; in manners civil and inoffensive, except when inebriated, as he too often was, by the donations of travellers and military officers, on which occasions he was frequently conveyed home in a single-wheeled chariot to the no small amusement of boys and adults. Briefly, he was at heart a man of genuine integrity and independence of soul; and, so far, poor Purslow has left thousands of survivors who are not his equals.'

[From the *Monthly Magazine*.]

THE CHURCH PREEN MODEL
OF A GALLANT HUNTING SQUIRE

Harry Sparrow (1824-1919)

Life in nineteenth-century Shropshire was dominated by squires and parsons. Harry Sparrow was an outstanding example of a hunting squire with the reputation of a daredevil horseman.

His family had made money in the iron-making industry in Staffordshire since 1500, and rebuilt Church Preen Manor on the grand scale. Harry was born in 1824 and began hunting with the Albrighton hounds at the age of six. His passion for the pastime kept him an active participant until he was eighty. He also hunted with other packs—the Cheshire, Worcestershire and Wheatland. Even after this he was involved in judging horses and show-jumping.

As a young man he lived in South America for ten years and was much admired for his superb horsemanship. He claimed to have made friends with 'Buffalo Bill' (William Cody) and he brought home with him a prairie wolf, which he used to take with him on rides.

In England again he worked in the family business on a basis which gave him plenty of time to indulge in popular sports—cricket, boxing and shooting. He was an officer in the Staffordshire Volunteers, retiring with the rank of captain at forty-two.

Like Mytton, he was once madcap enough to set a pair of horses harnessed to a gig at a turnpike gate. But he didn't get off so lightly. The Stanhope was smashed and the doughty squire regained consciousness only after two weeks. Later in his career he claimed to have broken nearly every bone in his body.

His most original feat was to ride an elephant into the Wrekin Hotel at Wellington. The animal had killed its keeper on the previous day. On another occasion he rode a horse up the Stoneway Steps in Bridgnorth and on yet another he rode around the dangerous Great Orme's Head at Llandudno.

Even more imaginatively, or foolishly, according to your point of view, he rode on consecutive days up a steep slope to the top of a blast furnace at Russell's Hall works and circled it several times amidst the flames and smoke.

Why did he take on such crazy challenges? Almost certainly for a wager, and to bolster and sustain his reputation as a rider who knew no fear. Unlike Mytton (*q.v.*), he did not go over the top with wild gambling and excessive drinking. In contrast with the Halston squire's wretched last days and demise at the tragically early age of thirty-seven, Sparrow died at home at ninety-five.

A MISER
FROM MADELEY AND MARKET DRAYTON

Sam Stretch (1732-1804)

This native of Market Drayton, who had seen active service in the Army as a young man, represents a classic case of the miser who ekes out a living in misery and apparent hardship, but turns out to have been better off than many of those who pitied him. His bequests might have surprised the beneficiaries by their nature and detail.

After his death at Madeley in 1804 the following obituary appeared in the *London Review or Literary Journal*.

'For a length of time he resided in an obscure building in Madeley, into which, it is said, he has not for many years admitted either male or female, and from the best account we can give it was indeed a dwelling of complete wretchedness. It is about fifteen years since he purchased a load of coals, a part of which was left at the time of his death.

'His chief employ was to go about to the adjacent towns, carrying letters and small parcels, and doing errands for his neighbours. His person bespoke the most abject penury. He usually appeared in an old slouched hat, and tattered garments scarcely sufficient to cover his nakedness, with a ragged bag hung over his shoulder, in which he mostly carried a little parsley, or some other kind of herb, the produce of his garden; these he generally offered as a present at the different places where he had to do business, and when accepted he took care to deal them out with a very sparing hand. This show of generosity, together with his eccentric dress and conversation, usually produced him a tenfold return.

'On searching his tattered satchel after his death it was found to contain old bones and shoe soles, pieces of paper, etc., which articles he usually collected in his peregrinations. His stock of linen consisted of two old shirts and a pair of sheets; in his hut were found several articles of silver plate, etc.

'His death was occasioned by a violent cold, brought on by his falling into a ditch in a state of intoxication on his return from Newcastle the Saturday preceding. By his penurious disposition he had amassed a considerable sum of money (exclusive of a loss of £500, which we understand he experienced a few years ago), a part of which he has left to purchase an additional bell for the church at Madeley, and an annual salary for it to be rung every night at nine o'clock during the summer months and eight during the winter; a chandelier for the church; a bell for the use of the free school; £5 per annum towards the organist's salary of that place, and a like annual amount for the Drayton organist; a further sum to be applied to the enlarging and repairing the Madeley almshouse, and clothing and educating two poor children until a proper age to be put apprentice; and to his relations two shillings and sixpence each.'

THE ROYAL JESTER FROM CONDOVER

Richard Tarlton (c1530-1588)

Richard Tarlton had greatness thrust upon him. According to the best-known account of his origin, he was born at Condover. The story goes that the youth was a funny-looking cove, with a squashed nose and a bad squint. While he was seeing to a farmer's pigs one day, a passer-by asked the way. The lad's quirky answers, in a rich Shropshire dialect, so entertained the traveller that he reported the interview with the comical swineherd to his master, who happened to be the Earl of Leicester. The nobleman wanted to see and hear for himself, so Richard was brought to London.

He was an instant success. Not only were his appearance and his speech entertaining in themselves, but he turned out to have a natural talent for repartee, comic acting and impromptu verse.

In 1583, he was invited to be a member of the Twelve Queen's Players, a group to which Shakespeare later belonged. Richard became a great favourite with Elizabeth I. He was always on call to cheer her up with his witty observations which became sarcastic when directed at those beyond the queen's circle of sycophants.

Some Shakespearian scholars are convinced that he was the 'poor Yorick' whose disinterred skull provoked Hamlet's philosophical musings.

Eventually, he had a tavern in Paternoster Row and then in Gracechurch Street. His personality and range of comic 'turns' drew customers from far and wide. Throughout the country, inns were named after him with the familiar portrait, with clay pipe and tabor, on the signboard.

Sadly Richard's success led to dissipation. He died in poverty and his body was buried at St Leonard's, Shoreditch.

A VERSATILE PEDESTRIAN

John Thomas (1822-?)

In the middle of the nineteenth century, before athletics had become an organised and popular sport, a Shrewsbury athlete named John Thomas attracted large crowds with his all-round athletic skills. He was principally a fast walker, or, as it was then called, a pedestrian, and pedestrianism, nothing to do with the modern, gently-moving confusion of Pride Hill, was the name of his game.

In order to attract interest, and no doubt earn a litle income for himself and for the numerous punters of those days, he issued a poster announcing a 'monster match', of man against time, the man being, of course, the confident Mr Thomas. For a wager of £100 to £50, he declared that he was prepared to walk 'fair heel and toe' sixty miles in twelve hours, for six consecutive days. He proposed to start at six a.m. on a Monday morning and finish at six on the following Saturday evening, and his daily stint would be to walk from the Lion and Pheasant Inn, on Wyle Cop, to the Haygate Inn, Wellington, and back, three times on each day.

This was not John's first venture into public athletics. He had, he claimed, demonstrated his speed and power as a pedestrian in London and the Provinces and had beaten a number of leading pedestrians, all named, including one G. Seward, the American Wonder.

Unhappily for Mr Thomas, his monster effort came to grief on the very first day. 'The cause of his failiure', a press notice explained, 'is wholly attributed to his injudiciously attempting the Task by walking in a new pair of shoes which so lacerated his Toes, and also caused his Feet to

Blister and Swell, as to render it fruitless to persevere longer . . .'

Almost at once he was beseeching friends for help. He had so crippled himself, he confessed, that for a time he would be unable to follow any occupation.

John's next trick was to offer a whole barrel of athletic feats within a given time. This is what he set himself to do in one and a half hours before a disappointingly meagre crowd on the Cricket Field adjoining the Armoury on a wet October 1st, 1849: walk one mile, run a mile, walk backwards a mile, hop 400 yards, pick up 40 stones placed a yard apart, clear 50 steeplechase hurdles, pull a gig a mile, pick up 50 eggs, placed a yard apart, with his mouth and convey them to a basket without breaking one or using his hands, and throw twelve 56 lb. weights over his head.

He spent Christmas Eve, 1849, taking part in a walking match against a man called Spooner, from Turnham Green. The course was a measured mile from the Column to the top of Emstrey Bank. A 'large concourse' of people turned up, many of whom had backed the local favourite. Alas! Mr Spooner, who was only eighteen while Thomas was pushing twenty-seven, won easily.

Fifteen months later John is reported taking part in another walking match, this time against Samuel Peaton, for £15 a side. For some reason, the stake has diminished with time. The course was seven miles between Shrewsbury and Atcham, milestone to milestone. The Shrewsbury man won, covering the distance in fifty-four minutes, fifty-seven seconds, no mean achievement, but his glory was a little tarnished, perhaps, when his opponent failed to finish, having suffered from stomach cramps before the end of the first mile. There was some doubt about the distance, so John walked an extra 660 yards, finishing, the report said, 'quite undistressed'.

A RESPECTED WRITER ON RURAL SHROPSHIRE

Mary Webb (1881-1927)

The novelist and poet was a nature-lover and a mystic, but her work sold only sluggishly until a Prime Minister's praise brought it to national attention. Throughout her rather short life she was absorbed in the Shropshire countryside.

Mary Webb lived at Leighton, Much Wenlock, Meole Brace, Pontesbury, Bayston Hill and, for a time, at Stanton-on-Hine-Heath. With a charming, easy-going father, whom she loved, and a somewhat overbearing mother, Mary inherited elements of both characters. She suffered from an over-active thyroid gland, which subjected her to recurring bouts of illness and depression. Only her independent spirit and compulsive drive to write enabled her to produce six novels, a lot of poetry and a volume of essays.

Mary married schoolmaster Henry Webb in 1912, much against the wishes of her fiancé's family. She listed seventy guests to be invited, mainly old ladies from the local workhouse, and including an organ-grinder, a herbalist and a one-eyed beggar. Her bridesmaid was the gardener's three-year-old daughter.

During the first world war, when the couple were living in Pontesbury, Henry had given up teaching and they were endeavouring to live on Mary's earnings, her £100 allowance, and what they could make from selling garden produce. Seeing this as a real contribution to the war effort, Mary would trudge the 14-mile return journey to Shrewsbury market with a basket of vegetables to sell. She and her husband were not too proud to hawk their surplus produce from door to door in Pontesbury, but their neighbours considered this practice on the part of well-to-do and educated people very odd indeed.

Later on, when royalty payments were coming in, Mary displayed a startling generosity to any tramp or beggar who approached her. It became her object to give a Christmas present to every child in her neighbourhood. To ensure the best results, she sent around a list for children to write down their requests. Some parents, suspicious of the strange pair, would have nothing to do with it. In other cases, Mary did her best to meet all demands, leading sometimes to great disparity in the value of gifts to the families concerned—for example, a piano to one and a doll to the child next door. Whenever Mary herself did the choosing, the resulting presents were often quite unsuitable, such as a sewing-box for a twelve-year-old boy. Mary tried to keep this scheme going even when she and her husband had moved to London, and always tended to give away more than she earned.

THE LONG-DISTANCE SWIMMER
FROM DAWLEY

Matthew Webb (1848-1883)

Born the son of a general practitioner, Webb showed an early aptitude for getting wet. Tales are told of his resource in rescuing his brother from drowning, and his daring in teetering along the parapet of Buildwas bridge.

In 1860 he began preparing for the Merchant Navy on the training-ship *Conway*, on the Mersey, where he registered another life-saving act, then joined a company trading with Far Eastern countries. Later, he became captain of the steamship *Emerald*, but resigned after six months with the intention of preparing for a cross-Channel swim.

His first attempt failed because of bad weather. The second, begun on the 24th August, 1875, ended successfully the next day and took 21¾ hours. Webb had swum a total distance of nearly forty miles, testimony to the difficulties presented by the tides and currents.

The exhausted swimmer was put to bed in a Calais hotel, and the patron summoned the local band to trumpet a hero's welcome outside his window. The hero rose wearily from his slumber and ungraciously told the musicians where he would like them to go.

Webb was received in England, and especially in Shropshire, with immense acclaim. He lectured all around the country, and received a handsome testimonial award which was capable of producing an annual income of £87. However, as the months went by, public adulation diminished. His glory began to fade.

Even though there were several well-publicised races against world-class swimmers, mostly in America, Webb needed success to draw crowds to his exhibitions. Back at home, Webb went in for a sixty-hour float in a steel tank, made originally to contain a whale, at Westminster. Thousands of people went to see him, but there was a growing opinion that this kind of exhibitionism was degrading for a former national hero.

By 1883, Webb was becoming desperate. A grand gesture was needed. He announced his intention of swimming the rapids and whirlpool in Niagara river below the Falls. But the foolhardy adventure resulted in tragedy. Battered mercilessly among the rocks of the rapids, he disappeared almost at once in the whirlpool. Four days later a boating bricklayer spotted his lifeless body.

A STALWART CAMPAIGNER
AGAINST DRUNKENNESS AND VICE

Julia Wightman (1815-1898)

The daughter of an Army lieutenant-colonel from Bath,
Julia married the Rev. Charles Edward Leopold Wightman,
vicar of St Alkmund's, Shrewsbury, and grandson of a
Russian prince, in 1842. Her parents opposed the union on
the grounds that Julia was not strong enough for the work
of a parson's wife, and that the pair were temperamentally
ill-matched.

Mrs Wightman proved them wildly wrong by devoting
much of the next fifty years to a sustained and successful
attempt to improve the lot of the poor and underprivileged.
Instead of merely busying herself in the parish work among
the respectable members of her husband's congregation, she
deliberately sought out the weak and the wicked, the drunk
and the dirty, the felon and the prostitute, and did her best
to show them a better way of life. She carried out much of
her work in the evenings, visiting the poor in their homes,
talking to people in the streets and inviting them to meetings
for Bible-study and prayer.

At first citizens were shocked to see her out, alone, at
night. Once she was reported having been seen in the
company of a notorious poacher. She found her subjects
mainly in the squalid areas of the town, places like Roushill
and Butcher Row.

She soon realised that the besetting evil of the oppressed
poor was strong drink. She tackled this problem by forming
'The St Alkmund's Total Abstinence Society'. She gave up
alcohol herself *pour encourager les autres*, and disposed of all
the vicarage beer.

Her book, *Haste to the Rescue*, sold well beyond the shores of Britain. With the proceeds she formed the C. of E. Temperance Society and bought the land for the erection of the Working Men's Hall, where Dyas's now stands.

In the 1850s she organised excursions for the members of the Total Abstinence Society. They went as far afield as Liverpool, but also visited Sutton Coldfield, Llanymynech, Ludlow, Grinshill and Hawkestone. Transport could involve trains, waggonettes and canal boats. These outings were very popular, and many people preferred joining them to going to the Show, where drunkenness and general mayhem were rife. One of her excursions could attract 800 participants.

She never skimped her parish duties. Her work among the poor and homeless people led to their bringing in friends from other parishes, which in turn drew complaints from the clergy. Julia's answer was to advise them to adopt her methods.

Early in her 'ministry', she belonged to a committee which opened the Salop Penitentiary, a refuge for fallen women. The object was to help women who were poor and homeless.

It is recorded that when her husband lay on his deathbed she sat beside him sewing her widow's weeds. When she felt that her own death was near, she made out cards reading 'Mrs Wightman entered into her rest this day—' leaving room for the date to be put in at the appropriate time. She was so universally loved that it is little wonder that her host of admirers ignored her request that she should not be given a public funeral.

THE MAN OF IRON

John Wilkinson (1727-1808)

There was a rumour that John Wilkinson was born in a cart on the way to market. His career was to be characterised by this individual approach to life.

He was a famous and successful ironmaster. One of his houses was at Broseley, and he played a leading part in public life and industrial development in east Shropshire. Although he was born in quite poor circumstances, his restless energy ensured personal advancement as an entrepreneur. Marrying into money helped the process forward.

He was popular with his workforce, and appeared to have the welfare of his employees very much at heart. But he was conceited, held unorthodox religious views and was not morally impeccable. (He believed that sexual intercourse was a sovereign cure for indigestion, to which he was a martyr.)

He built the first blast furnace in Bilston, launched the first iron boat in 1787, and was connected with the erection of the famous iron bridge. He was the first to use a steam engine for supplying air directly to a blast furnace, and improved the manufacture of the cannon.

His domestic life was less well-regulated. His daughter was anxious to marry a Shropshire clergyman named Theophilus Holbrooke, whom her father found unacceptable. She insisted, was cut off with a shilling, and he never spoke to her again. She died in the following year. She was buried, despite the estrangement, in the garden at Castlehead, a large house built for Wilkinson at Grange-over-Sands. For some reason, perhaps connected with the fact that Castlehead was frequently cut off by the tide, her body was moved five times. Eventually her father planted a gooseberry bush on the final grave.

Wilkinson requested in his will that he be buried in an iron coffin in one of three places, Castlehead being one of them. Growing capricious with advancing age, Wilkinson had several coffins of varying sizes made. These were hidden among trees at Castlehead and it amused him to take visitors to 'choose their coffin'.

He died in Staffordshire at the age of eighty. His body was put into wooden and lead coffins and taken to Castlehead, where it was found that the shells would not fit fit into the special iron coffin. The cadaver was set aside while a larger coffin was made. Then a bed of rock beneath the surface at the designated spot for the grave made it impossible to bury the large coffin deep enough. So once again the corpse had to be put by until enough rock had been removed for the hole to be of adequate depth.

An iron pyramid weighing twenty tons was erected over the grave, a short distance from the drawing-room window. Marketing the house in 1828, the owners decided that this memorial might detract from its value, so there was a clandestine exhumation and the body and its three coffins were taken up the hill to the chapel.

Apart from a huge fortune, John Wilkinson left behind three illegitimate children, the eldest of them only five, and the youngest fathered when this vigorous old individualist was seventy.

Selected Bibliography

'The Shropshire Magazine': various issues
'Country Quest': various issues
Watton, Cuttings.
Boreatton Park, Brown. (Brown, 1989)
Shrewsbury and Shropshire, Wrenn. (Longmans, 1968)
Mary Webb, Coles. (Billings, 1990)
Salopian Annals, Pidgeon.
The Church of St Michael the Archangel, Llanyblodwell, Purser.
Victorian Shrewsbury, ed. Trinder. Shropshire Libraries, 1984.
History of Oswestry, Cathrall. (Lewis, 1855)
Shropshire (Shell Guide), Moulder. (Faber & Faber, 1972)
The Industrial Revolution in Shropshire, Trinder. (Phillimore, 1973)
The Centenarians of the Andes, Davies. (Readers' Union, 1976)
Shropshire (King's England Series), Mee. (Hodder & Stoughton)
Shropshire County Guide. (British Publishing Co. Ltd., Glos.)
Shropshire. (S.C.C., 1980)
Shropshire, Herring. (Elek, 1949)
50 Shropshire Celebrities, Elderwick. (1989)
The History of Myddle, Gough, ed. Hey. (Penguin, 1981)
Borough of Much Wenlock, Lloyd. (B. C. of Much Wenlock)
The Book of Shrewsbury, de Saulles. (Barracuda, 1986)
The Welsh Border, Gibbons. (Geographia, Ltd. n.d.)
The Durants of Tong Castle, Jeffrey. (n.d.)
The Shropshire Village Book, W.I. (Countryside Books, 1988)
The River Severn, Kissack. (Dalton, 1982)
Portrait of Severn, Peel. (Hale, 1968)
Witches and Warriors, Lowe. (Shropshire Libraries, 1990)
The Life and Death of Jack Mytton, Esquire, Nimrod.
Follies (N. T. Guide), Headlay & Meulenkamp. (Cape, 1986)
Chambers Biographical Dictionary (1984)
Capt. Webb, Channel Swimmer, Elderwick (1987)
A Dictionary of British History, ed. Kenyon. (Secker & Warburg)
This is my Life, Hunt. (Blackie & Sons, n.d.)
Shropshire Hill Country, Waite. (Phillimore, n.d.)
A Glimpse of Old Shropshire, Austerberry. (Wilding, n.d.)